Contents

Macmillan Education
4 Crinan Street
London N1 9XW
A division of Springer Nature Limited

Companies and representatives throughout the world

Ferris Wheel 1 Activity Book ISBN 978-1-380-01869-4

First published 2019

Original design by Clare Webber
Page make-up by emc design ltd
Original character design by Jose Ignacio Gómez (Nacho Gómez)
Illustrated by BluBlu Animation Group Sp. z o.o. pp3–5, 7, 8, 12, 13, 15–19, 21, 23–25, 27–30, 31a,c, 33b, 35, 37, 38, 39b,d,f, 41, 42, 43b, 45–49, 52, 53, 55, 57, 58, 63–65, 66e–h, 67, 68, 72, 73b, 75–79, 82–96; Arpad Olbey (Beehive Illustration) pp6, 9–11, 14, 20, 22, 26, 31b,d, 32, 33a, 34, 36, 39a,c,e, 40, 43a, 44, 50, 51, 54, 56, 59–62, 66a-d, 69–71, 73a, 74, 80, 81
Cover design by emc design ltd
Cover illustration by Jose Ignacio Gómez (Nacho Gómez).

Authors' acknowledgements
I would like to thank everyone at Macmillan Education in the UK, Spain and Mexico who has contributed to the development and production of these materials. I would also like to thank all the teachers who have taken time to read and pilot the materials, and given invaluable feedback at every stage of writing the course. Special thanks as ever go to my husband, Alan, for his encouragement and support, and to our son and daughter, Jamie and Hannah, from whose early childhood days I learnt so much.

The publishers would like to thank Alex Tamulis, São Paulo, Brazil; Ayşegül Sezer, İNO Schools, Turkey; Daniela Araujo Pielli, Alt Idiomas, São Bernardo Do Campo, Brazil; Daniela Pugliese, Milton's College, Buenos Aires, Argentina; Esra Ezici, Turkey; Fernanda Domeniconi Nery Amorim, São Paulo, Brazil; Gabriela Iocolari, English Schoolhouse, Buenos Aires, Argentina; Gulbin Cin, Bahcesehir College, Turkey; Mariana Pastorino, Em Pi Instituto de Inglés, Santa Fe, Argentina; Mariné Ortiz, Warrington, Buenos Aires, Argentina; Paola Daniela Tuninetti, Academia Argüello, Córdoba, Argentina; Silvana Paola Accardo, Escuela Cooperativa Mundo Nuevo Instituto Casa de Jesús, Buenos Aires, Argentina.

Printed and bound in Brazil

2024
38

Hello
Welcome!

Point and say the names. Trace to circle Mimi and Dylan. Say.
Language: Mimi, Dylan; boy, girl; Hello, I'm (Mimi).

Color the circle for Mimi and Dylan in blue. Color the circle for Mommy and Daddy in red. Say.

Language: Mommy, Daddy, Mimi, Dylan; red, blue

Family
The Ferris Wheel

Trace to circle Daddy in yellow. Trace to circle Mommy in green. Trace to circle brother in red. Trace to circle sister in blue. Point and say.
Language: mommy, daddy, brother, sister; blue, green, red, yellow

Find and color Grandma and Grandpa. Ask and say.
Language: mommy, daddy, grandma, grandpa, brother, sister; Where's (grandma)? Here.

Color the pod with Dylan and Grandma yellow. Color the pod with Mimi and Grandpa orange. Ask and say.

Language: mommy, daddy, grandma, grandpa, brother, sister; Ferris Wheel; orange, yellow; Where's (Grandpa)? Here.

Story Song

Trace the Ferris Wheel going round. Color the pod you want to go in. Ask and say.

Language: Ferris Wheel; colors; Round and round. Where's (Mimi)? Here.

Draw and color you and your family. Ask and say.

Language: mommy, daddy, grandma, grandpa, brother, sister; Where's your (grandma)? Here. This is my (brother).

Lesson 6 Values I love my family

Color the circles to show the family members you love. Say.

Language: mommy, daddy, grandma, grandpa, brother, sister; I love my (brother).

Trace the wheels. Count and say.

Language: round, wheel; numbers 1–5; This is (a wheel). Wheels go round and round.

Draw your family or friends on the bus. Color the wheels. Point and say.
Language: mommy, daddy, grandma, grandpa, brother, sister; friend; bus, wheels;
The wheels on the bus go round and round.

Color the faces to show the family members you know. Ask and say. Think and color the stars to show your progress.
Language: mommy, daddy, grandma, grandpa, brother, sister; Where's your (sister)? Here. This is my (daddy).

Glue a photo or draw and color a picture of your family. Point, ask and say. Talk about your family. Language: mommy, daddy, grandma, grandpa, brother, sister; Where's your (grandpa)? Here. This is my (sister). I love my (daddy).

Classroom

Mimi's first day at school

Vocabulary Lesson 1

Color the classroom objects. Point and say.
Language: book, crayon, eraser, pencil

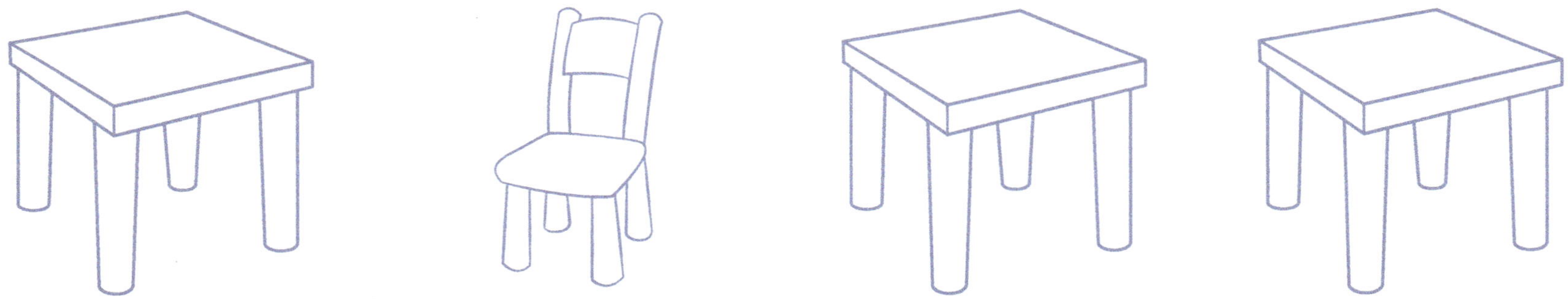

Point and say. Color the classroom object in each row that is different.
Language: book, chair, crayon, eraser, pencil, table; It's (a pencil).

Color Mimi's book, eraser, pencil and crayon. Point, ask and say.

Language: book, crayon, eraser, pencil; It's (a crayon). Where's your (book)? Here.

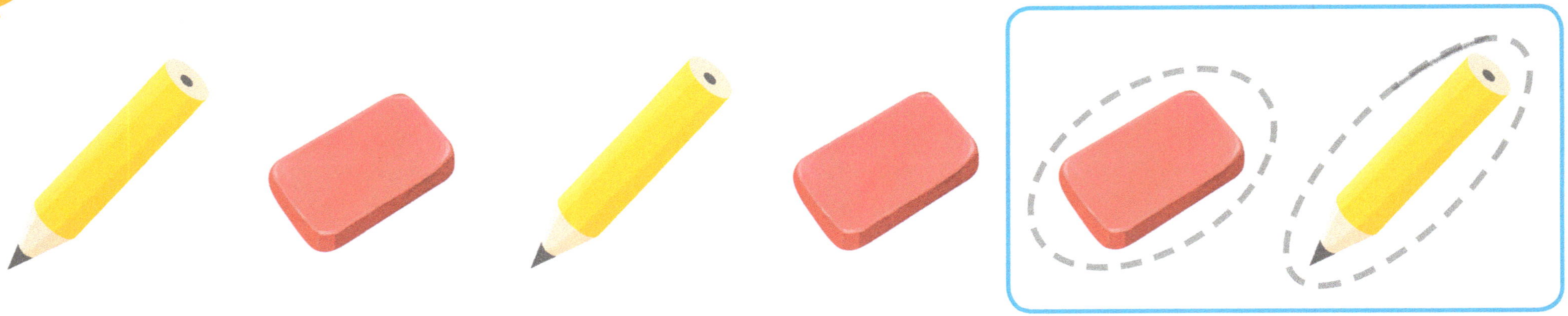

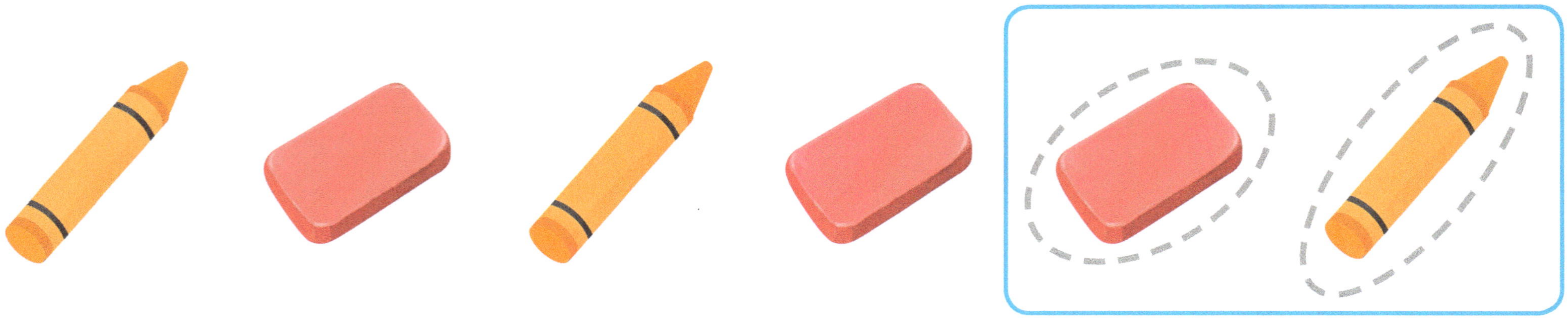

Point and say. Trace to circle the correct object to complete the sequence. Ask and say.
Language: book, crayon, eraser, pencil; Where's your (book)? Here.

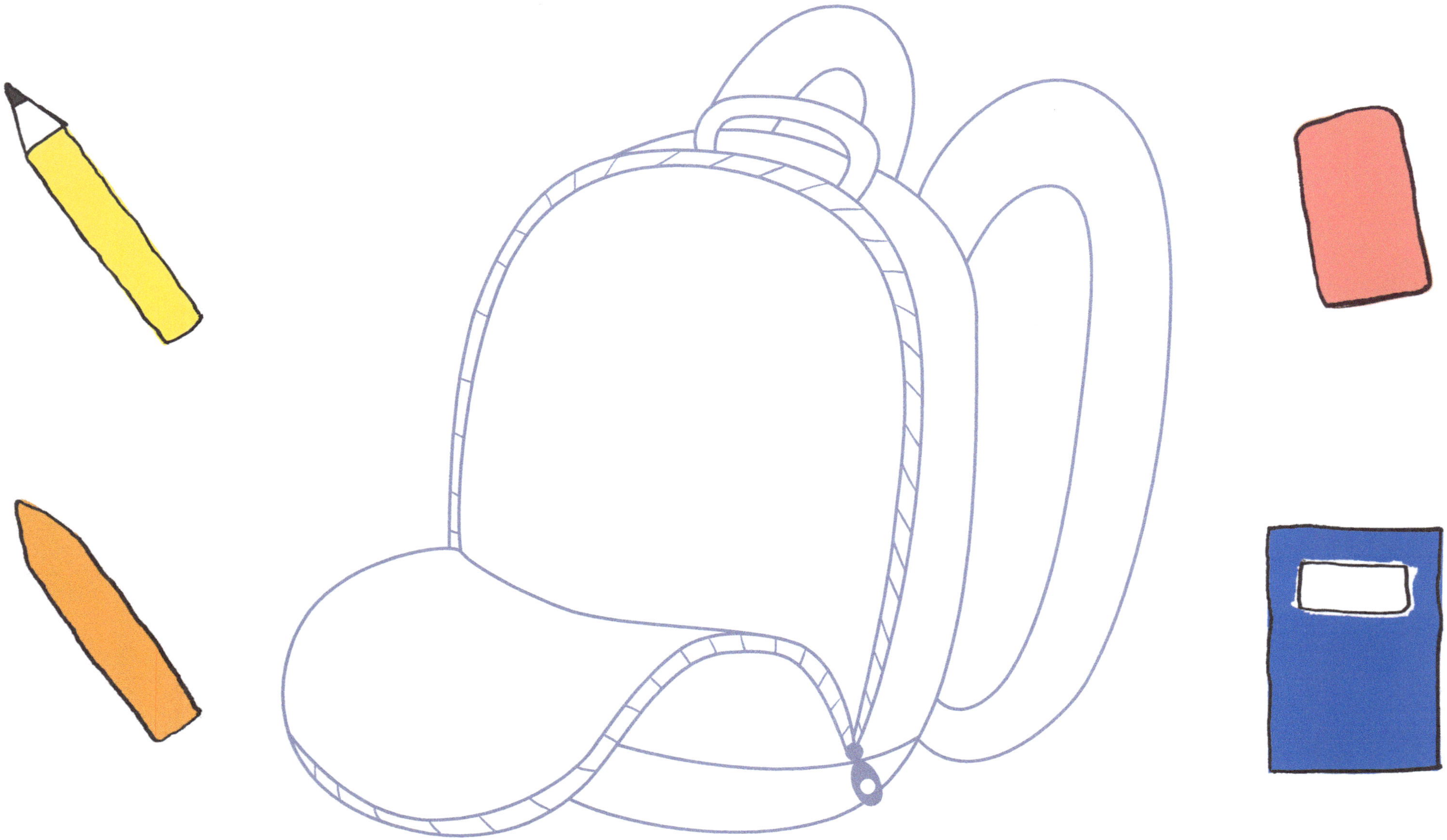

Draw and color the objects you take to school inside the backpack. Point, ask and say.
Language: book, crayon, eraser, pencil; colors; Where's your (book)? Here. What color is your (book)? It's (blue).

Color the frame of the happy friends yellow and the sad friend blue. Say.
Language: care, friend, happy, sad; I care. I'm your friend.

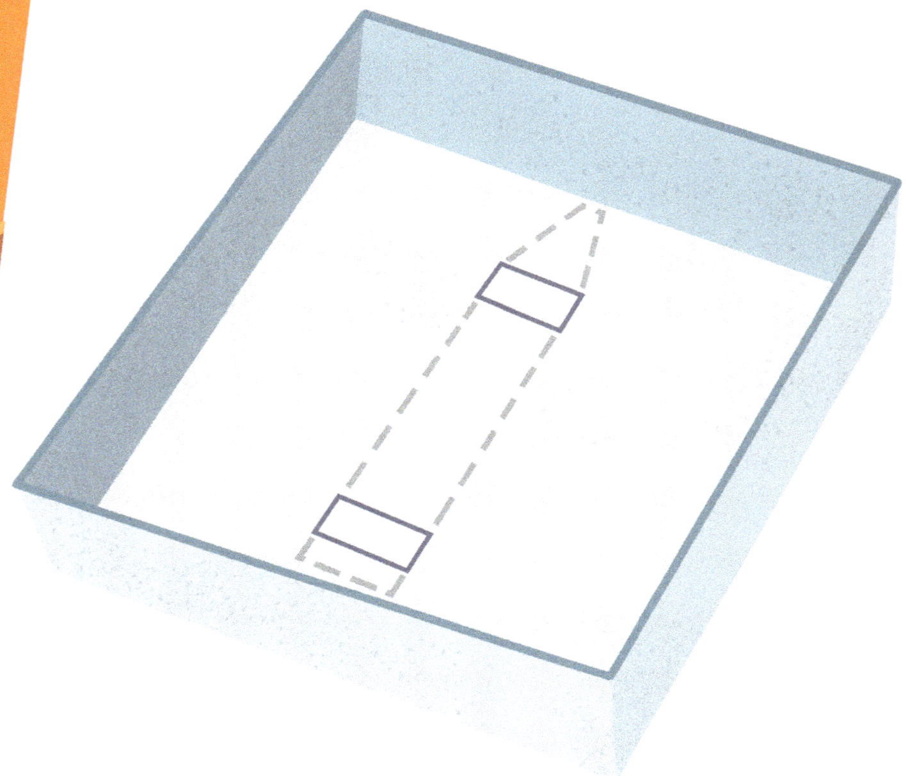

Trace the book and crayon where they belong. Say.
Language: book, crayon; shelf, tray; I put the (crayon) (in) the (tray).

Trace to match the children saying 'hello' and 'bye bye'. Point and say.
Language: bye bye, hello; friends, school; This is the way I say (hello).

Color the faces to show the classroom objects you know. Ask and say. Think and color the stars to show your progress.
Language: book, chair, crayon, eraser, pencil, table; colors; It's (a crayon). Where's your (book)? Here. What color is your (book)? It's (red).

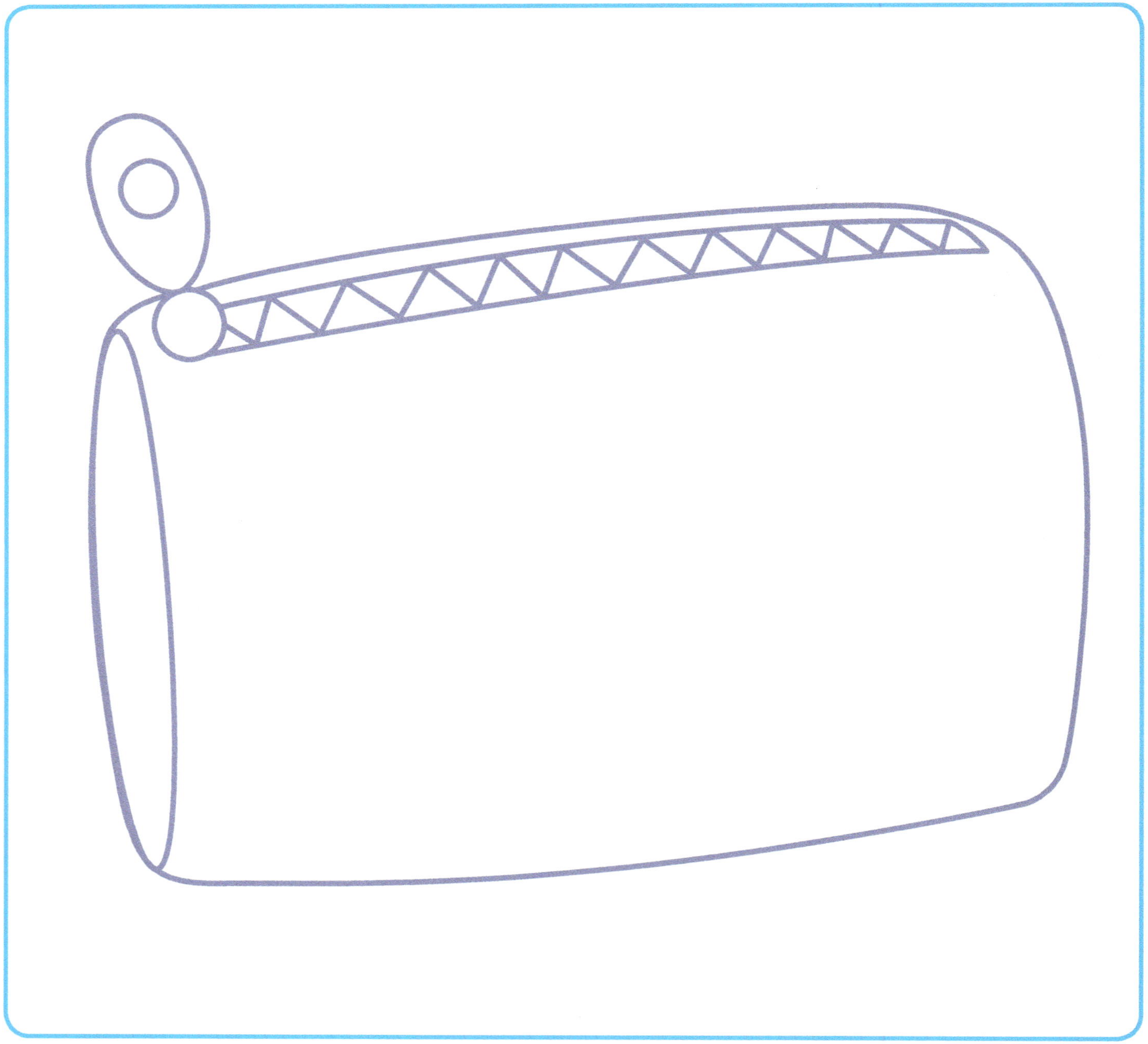

Draw and color objects to take to school. Count the objects. Point, ask and say.

Language: crayon, eraser, pencil; colors; numbers; It's (a pencil). Where's your (eraser)? Here. What color is your (pencil)? It's (blue).

My face

Splash!

Trace Dylan's eyes and mouth and Mimi's ears and nose. Point and say.
Language: ears, eyes, mouth, nose

Draw and color your hair. Trace the teeth and color your eyes. Point and say.
Language: ears, eyes, hair, mouth, nose, teeth; I have (hair).

Trace the paths to connect the story pictures in order. Color a circle to show your favorite picture in the story. Say.

Language: ears, eyes, mouth, nose; boy, girl; water; I have (two eyes). It's a (boy) in the water.

Story Song

Color Mimi's eyes and mouth and Dylan's ears and nose. Point and say.
Language: ears, eyes, mouth, nose; boy, girl; It's a (boy) in the water.

Life skills

Trace and color the ears, eyes, nose and mouth on the puppet. Point and say.
Language: ears, eyes, hair, mouth, nose; colors; I have an (orange) (nose).

My face

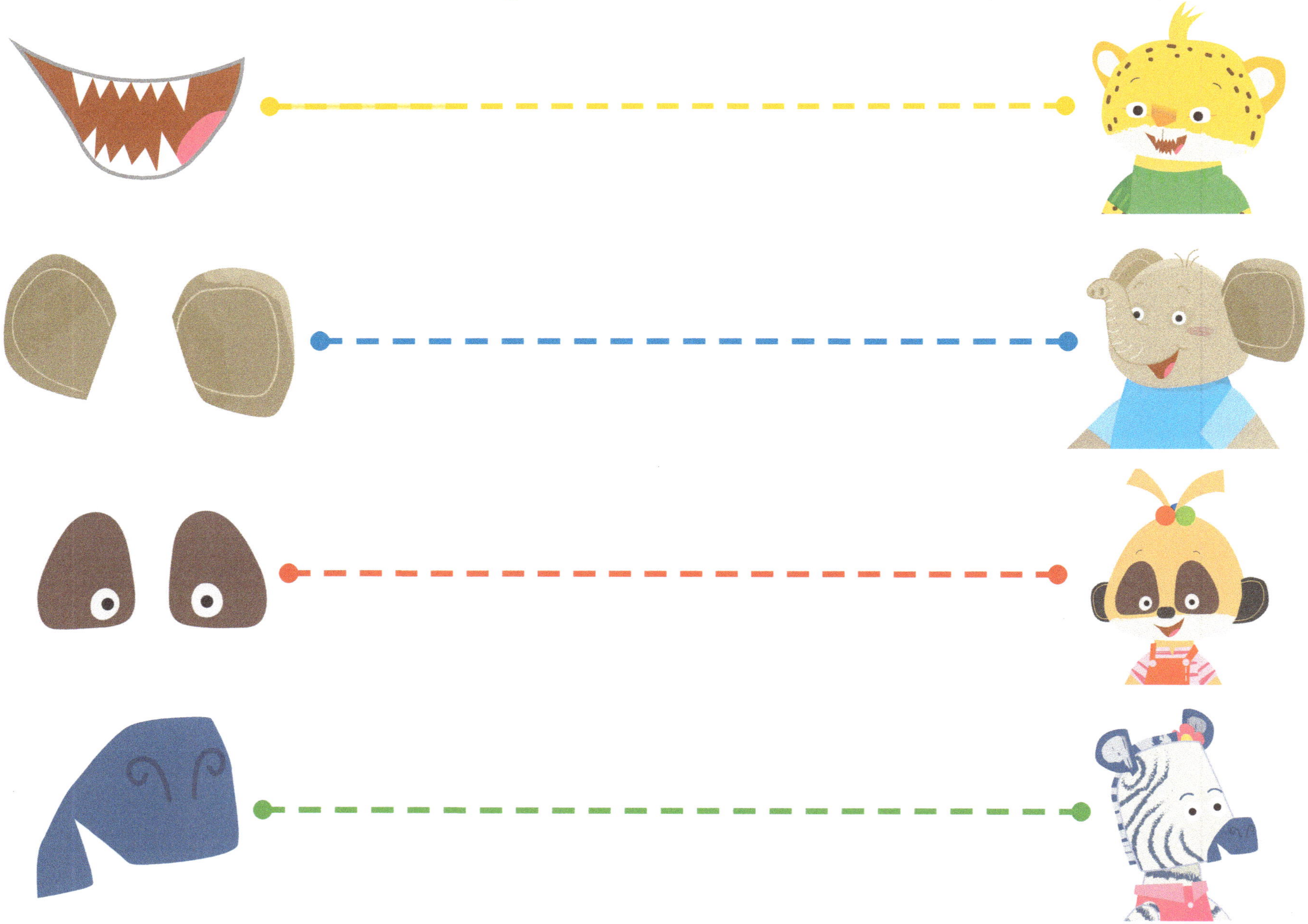

Point and say. Trace to match the parts of the face to the characters.

Language: ears, eyes, mouth, nose, teeth; happy, special

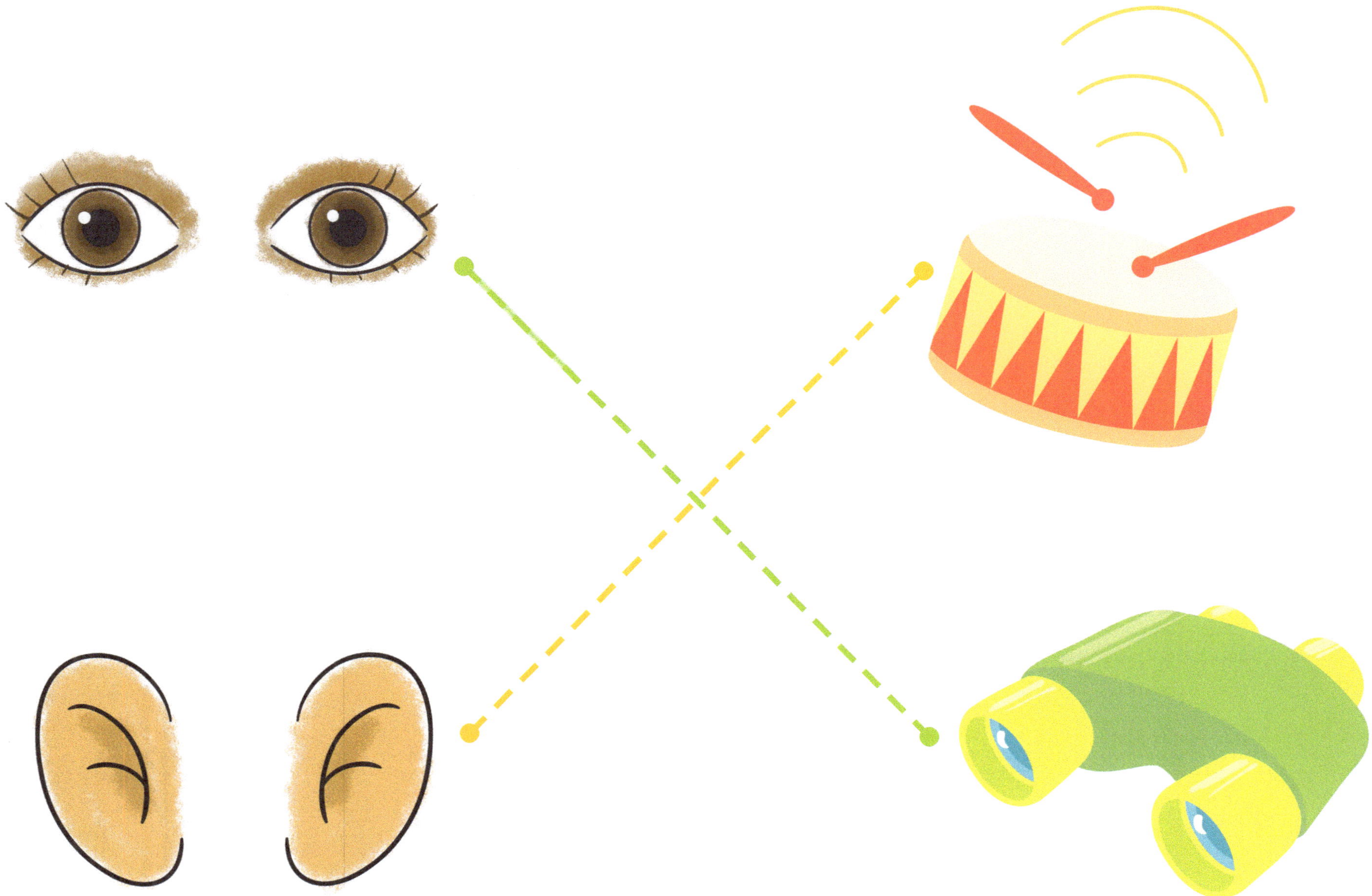

Trace to match. Point and say.
Language: hear, see; ears, eyes; I (see) with my (eyes).

Follow and draw paths to match the children showing the same body parts. Say.
Language: ears, hands, mouth, toes; Here is my (nose). Here are my (toes).

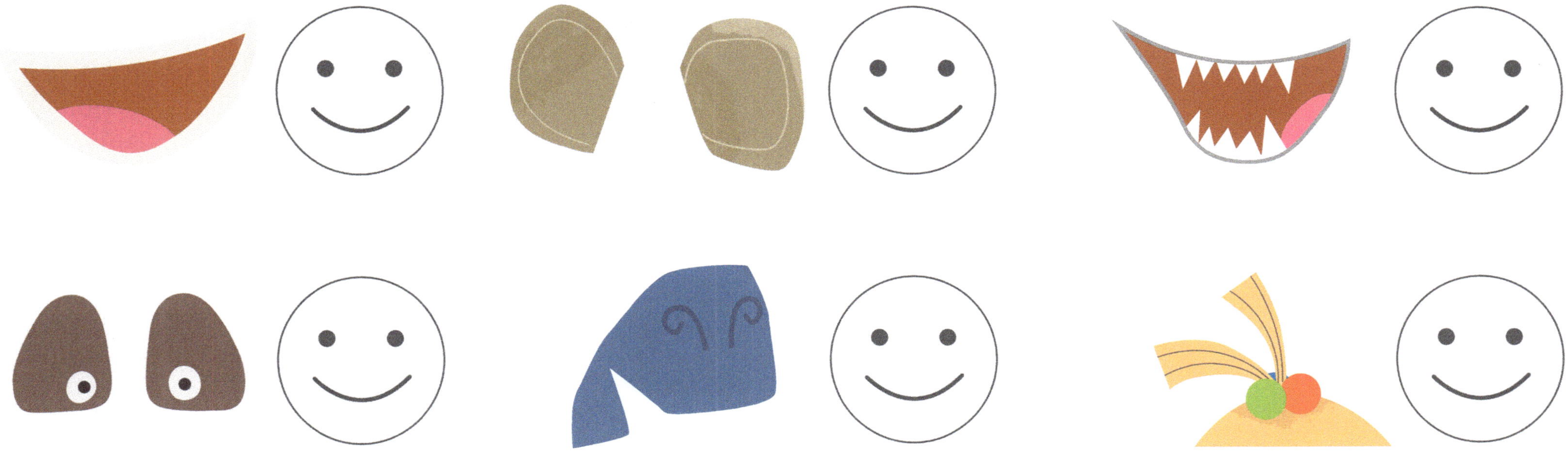

Color the faces to show the parts of the face you know. Point and say. Think and color the stars to show your progress.
Language: ears, eyes, hair, mouth, nose, teeth; I have (hair).

My face

Look in a mirror. Paint a picture of you. Point and say.

Language: ears, eyes, hair, mouth, nose, teeth; colors; numbers; I have (hair). I have (two) (blue) (eyes).

Clothes
Time to get dressed!

Vocabulary Lesson 1

Point and say. Color the clothes.
Language: hat, shoes, shorts, T-shirt

Point and say. Trace the coat and the boots and color the clothes.
Language: boots, coat, hat, shoes, shorts, T-shirt; Put on your (hat).

Color Dylan's clothes in the correct place. Point and say.
Language: hat, shoes, shorts, T-shirt; Put on your (hat).
Take off your (shorts).

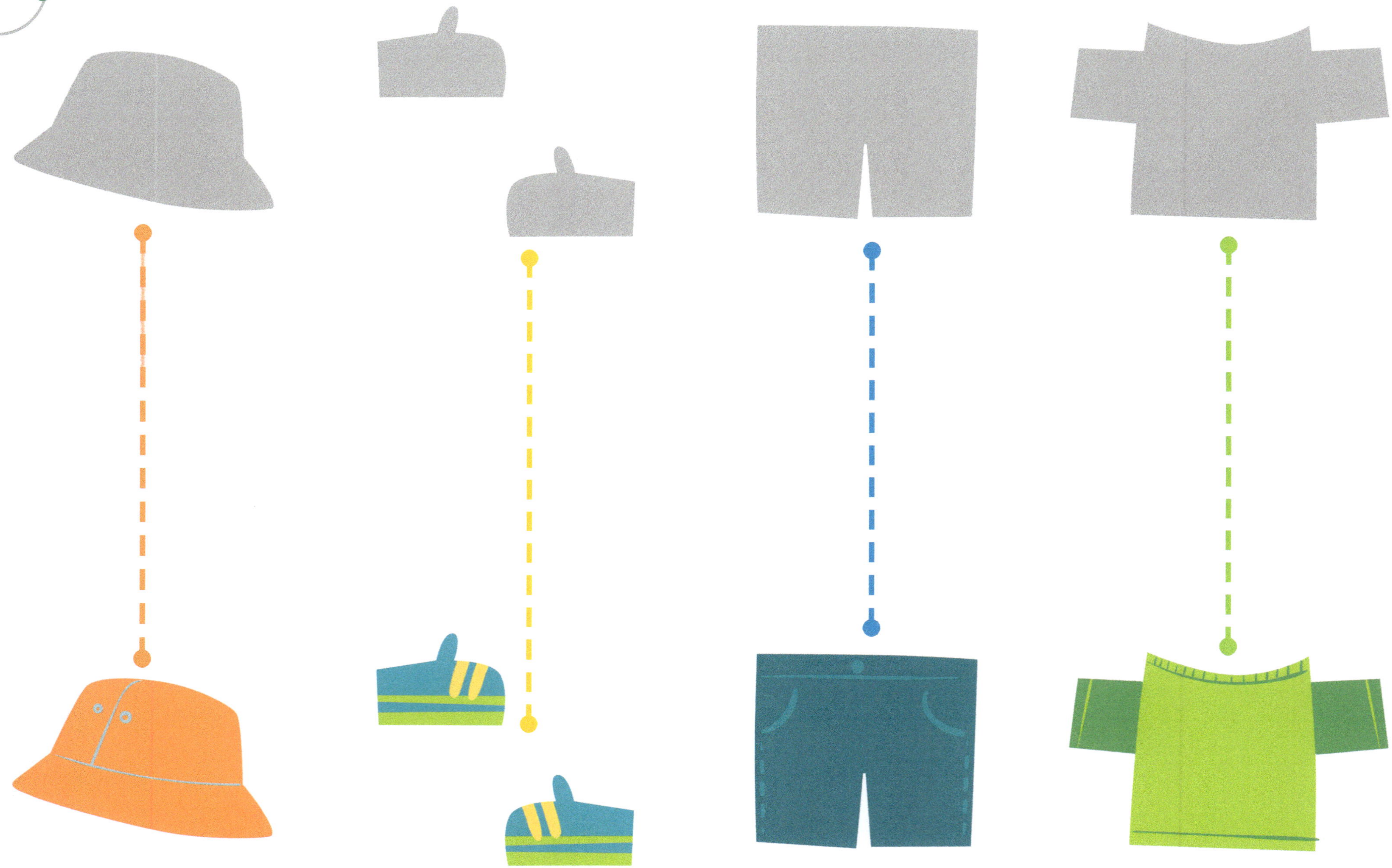

Trace to match Dylan's clothes. Ask and say.
Language: hat, shoes, shorts, T-shirt; Where are your (shorts)? Here.

Follow and draw paths to match the people to their clothes. Ask and say.
Language: boots, coat, hat; Where's your (coat)? Where are your (boots)? Here. Put on your (hat).

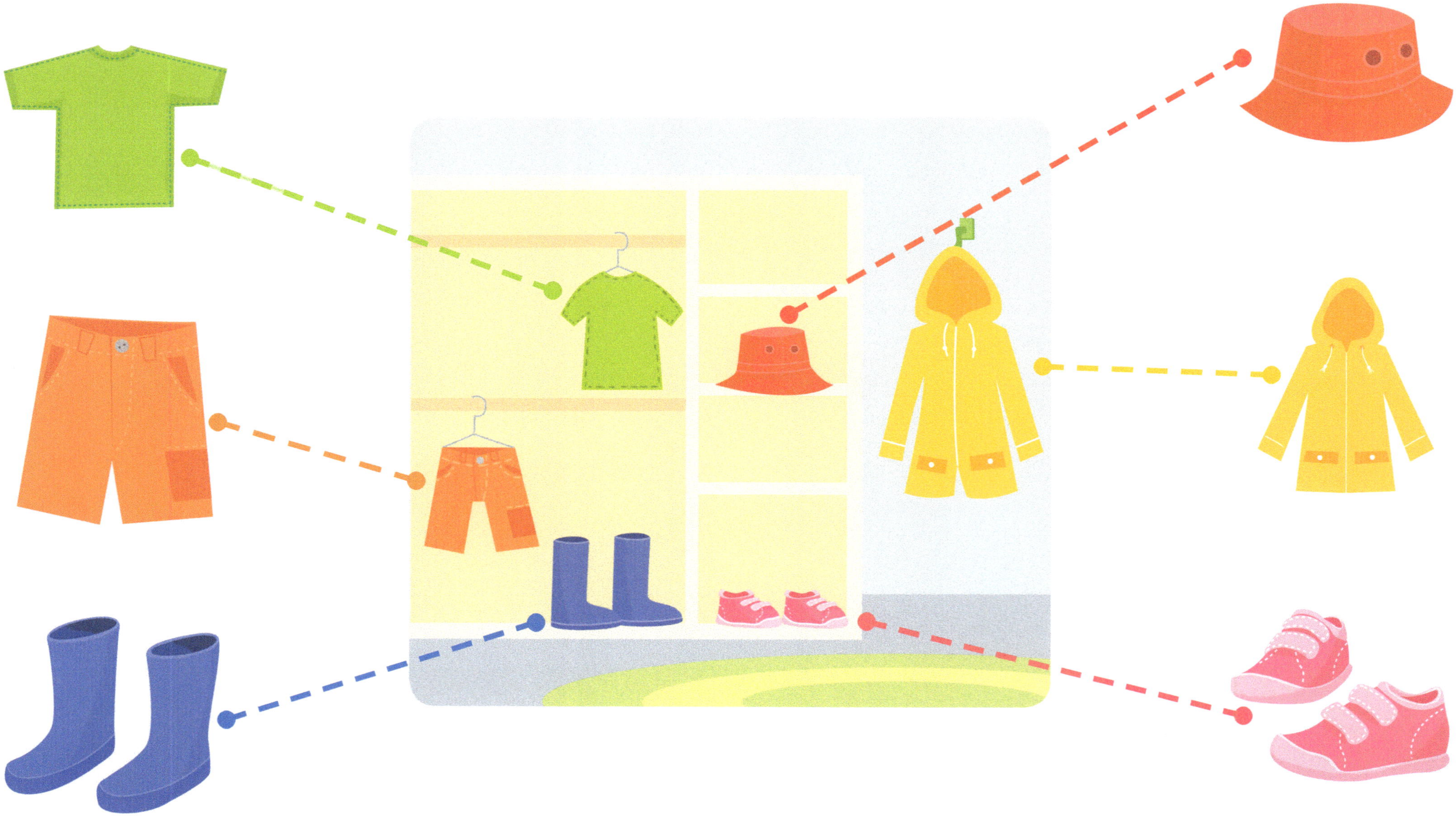

Trace to match the clothes to the correct place. Say.

Language: boots, coat, hat, shoes, shorts, T-shirt; neat; I'm neat. I put my (coat) away.

Circle the clothes for sunny weather in orange. Circle the clothes for rainy weather in blue. Say.
Language: boots, coat, hat, shoes, shorts, T-shirt; rainy, sunny; It's (rainy). I put on my (coat).

Trace and count the missing legs on the spider. Point and say.

Language: spider; rain, sun; numbers 1–4.

Color the faces to show the clothes you know. Ask and say. Think and color the stars to show your progress.
Language: boots, coat, hat, shoes, shorts, T-shirt; Put on your (hat). Take off your (coat). Where's your (T-shirt)? Where are your (shoes)? Here.

Project

Glue a photo or paint a picture of you in rainy or sunny weather. Point, ask and say.
Language: boots, coat, hat, shoes, shorts, T-shirt; rainy, sunny; colors; It's (rainy). I put on (a red) (coat). Where's your (hat)? Where are your (shorts)? Here. What color is your (coat)? It's (blue). What color are your (shorts)? They're (red).

Toys
The old toy box

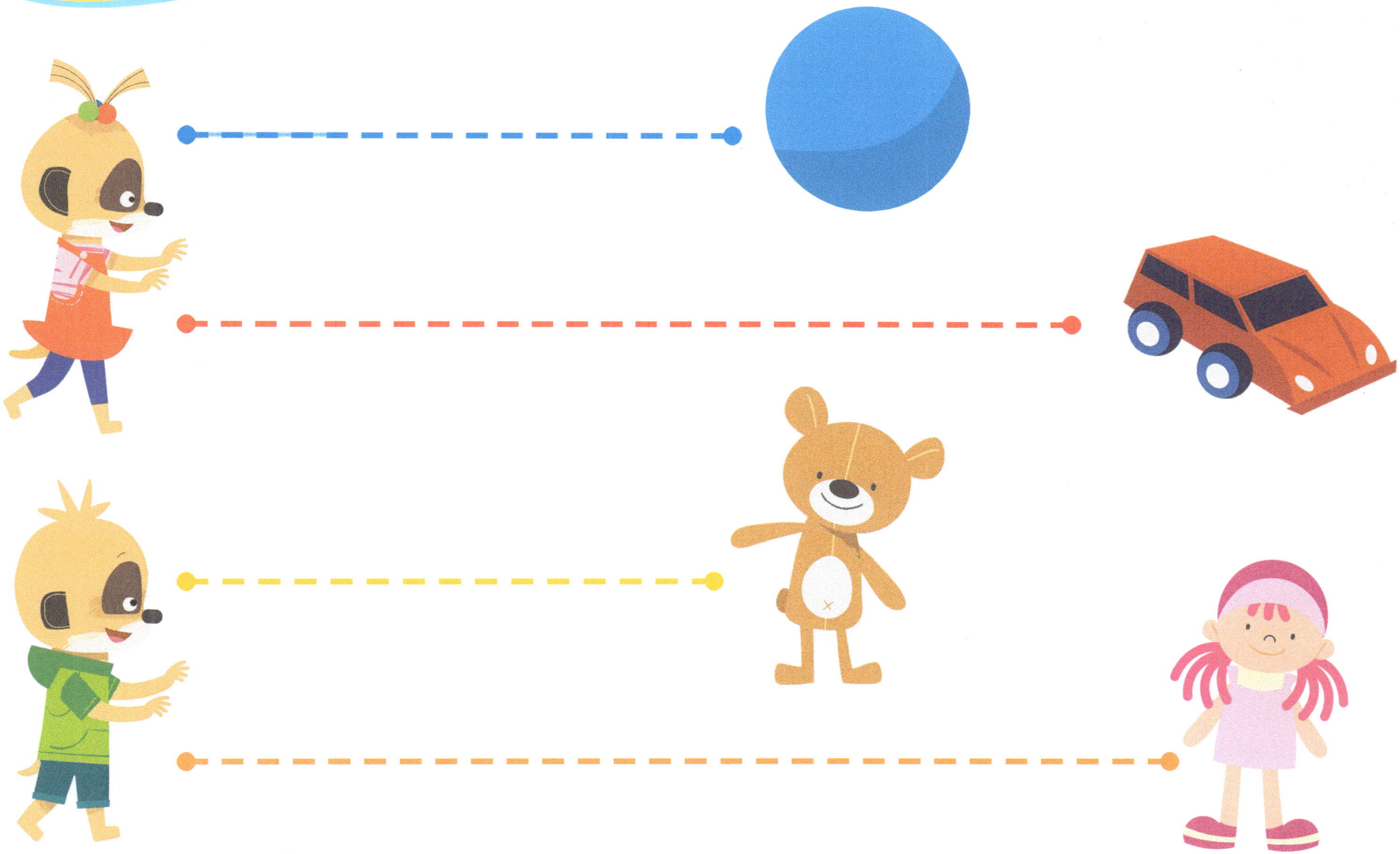

Trace to match Mimi and Dylan to the toys. Point and say.
Language: ball, car, doll, teddy

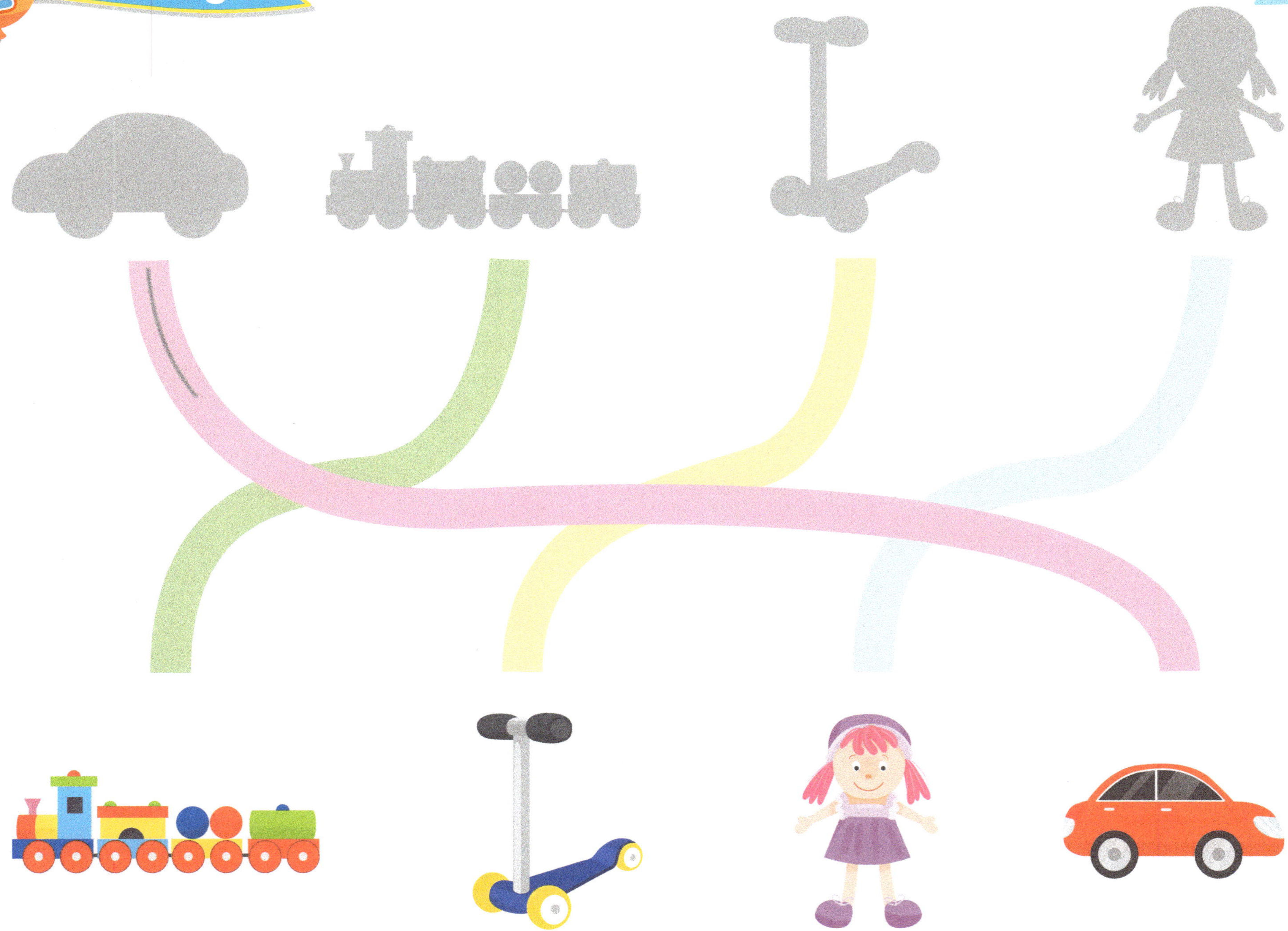

Follow and draw paths to match the toys. Point, ask and say.
Language: car, doll, scooter, train; What's this? It's (a car).

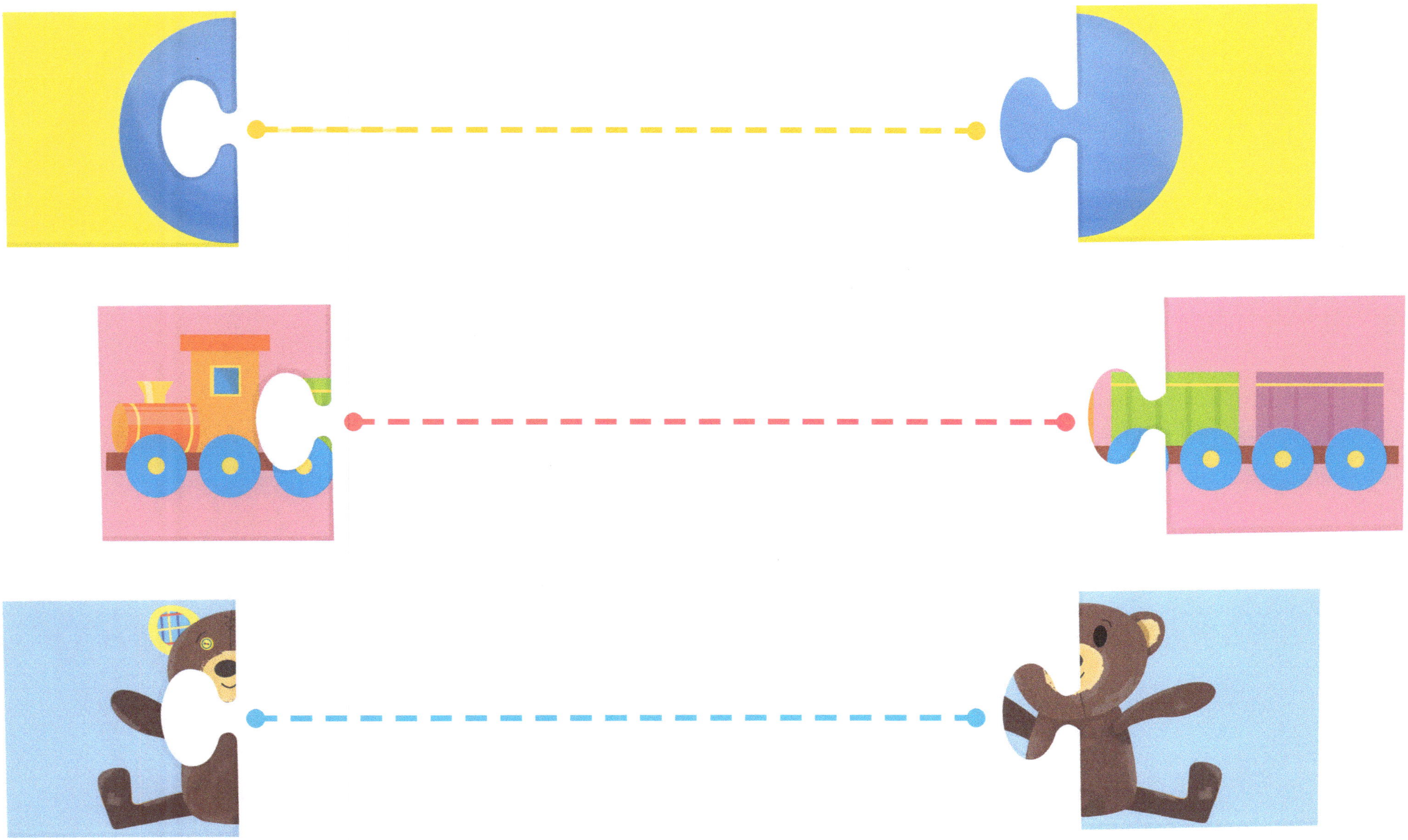

Trace to match the puzzle pieces. Point, ask and say.

Language: ball, teddy, train; What's this? It's (a train). Let's play with the (ball).

Choose and draw the toy you want to play with in the toy box. Color the toy. Point, ask and say.
Language: ball, teddy, train; What's this? It's (a train). Let's play with the (teddy).

Trace to circle your favorite toy in red. Ask and say. Trace to circle your friend's favorite toy in green.
Language: ball, car, doll, scooter, teddy, train; What's this? It's (a train). What's your favorite toy? It's (my scooter).

Color the circles to show how you play and work with your friends. Say.
Language: play, work; Let's (work) together.

Trace to circle your favorite classroom activity red. Trace to circle your favorite playground activity blue. Point and say.

Language: classroom, playground; play, work; I (play) in the (playground).

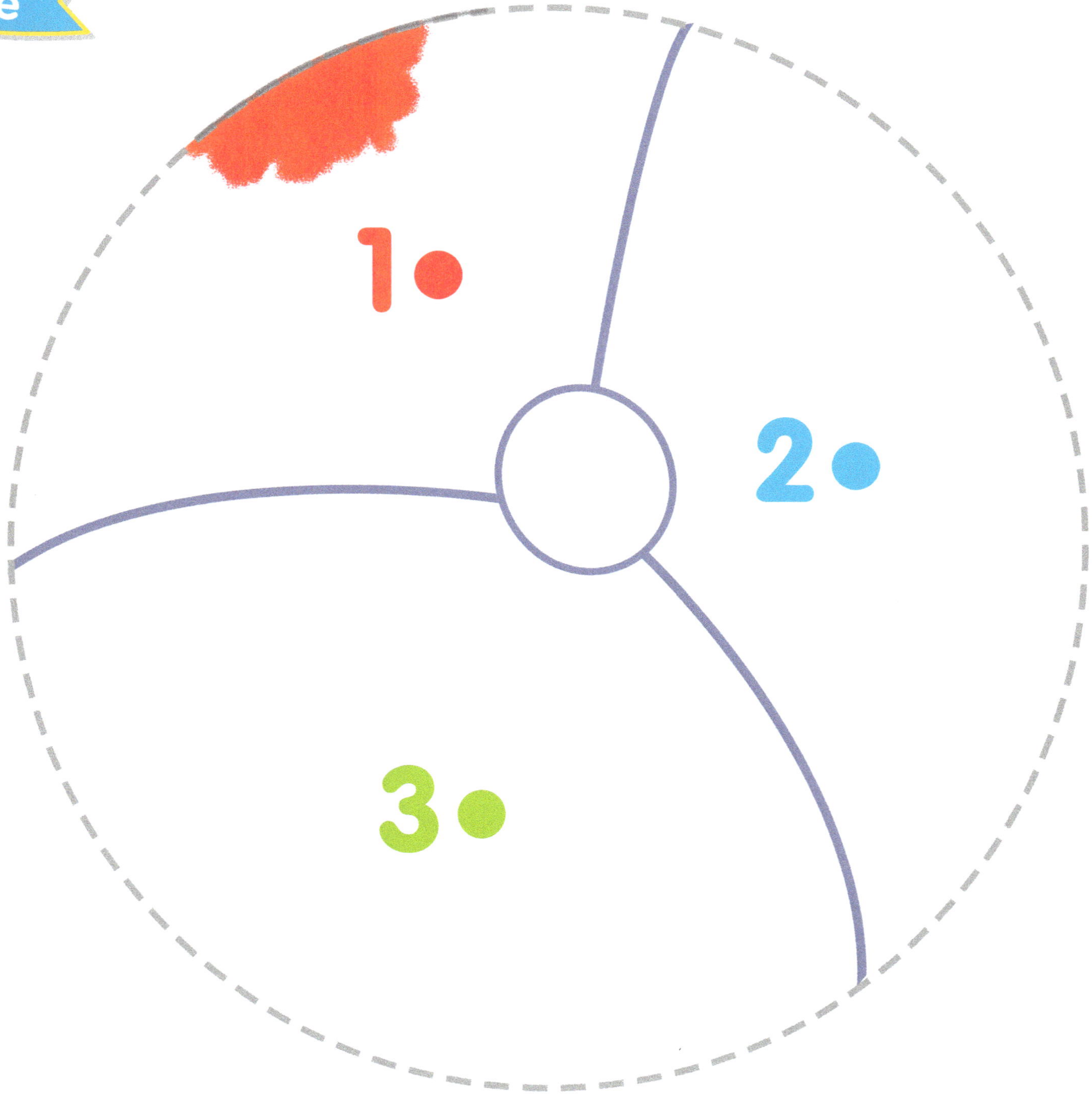

Trace the ball. Count and say. Color the ball red, blue and green.

Language: ball; big, round; colors; numbers 1–3

Color the faces to show the toys you know. Ask and say. Think and color the stars to show your progress.
Language: ball, car, doll, scooter, teddy, train; What's this? It's (a train). Let's play with the (car).
What's your favorite toy? It's (my ball).

Project

Find and glue pictures of toys. Point, ask and say.

Language: ball, car, doll, scooter, teddy, train; colors; What's this? It's (a teddy). Let's play with the (scooter). Where's the (car)? Here. It's (blue). What's your favorite toy? It's (my train).

Food

The picnic

Trace and color the food. Point and say.

Language: apple, banana, cookie, sandwich

Color the food and drink you like. Point and say.

Language: apples, bananas, cookies, juice, sandwiches, water; I like (juice).

Trace the paths to connect the story pictures in order. Color a circle to show your favorite picture in the story. Ask and say. Language: banana, cookie, juice, sandwich; I'm hungry. Can I have my lunch, please? Here's (a sandwich) for you. Thank you. I like (bananas).

Find and color the food in the lunchbox. Point and say.
Language: banana, cookie, sandwich; I'm hungry. Here's (a sandwich) for you. Thank you.

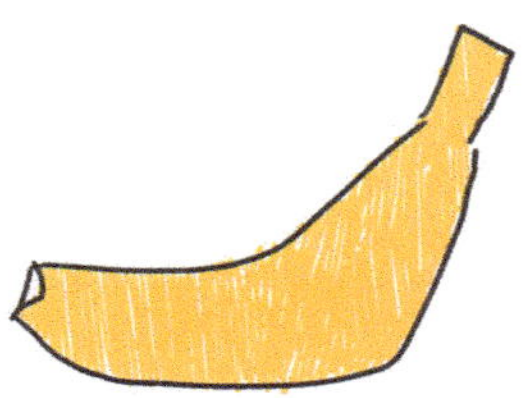

Choose and draw your picnic. Color. Ask and say.

Language: apple, banana, cookie, juice, sandwich, water; Are you hungry? Can I have (a sandwich), please? Here you go. Thank you. I like (bananas).

Values I say 'please' and 'thank you'

Draw pictures of you saying 'please' and 'thank you'. Point and say.
Language: please, thank you

SOCIAL AND EMOTIONAL LEARNING

Trace to match things we eat and things we drink. Say.

Language: drink, eat; apples, bananas, cookies, juice, sandwiches, water; I eat (apples). I drink (water).

Count the apples and oranges. Trace to circle the picture that is the same in each row. Point and say.

Language: apples, oranges; numbers 1–4

Color the faces to show the food you know. Ask and say. Think and color the stars to show your progress.
Language: apple, banana, cookie, juice, sandwich, water; I'm hungry. Are you hungry? Can I have (a cookie), please? Here you go. Here's (a banana) for you. Thank you. I like (sandwiches).

1 2 3 4 5

1 2 3 4 5

Paint the bananas and apples. Count and circle the correct number. Point, ask and say.
Language: apples, bananas; colors; numbers 1–5; I'm hungry. Can I have (a banana), please? Here you go. Thank you. I like (apples).

Pets
The little dog

Trace to match the body parts to the pets. Color the pets' body parts. Point and say.
Language: bird, fish, mouse, rabbit

Follow and draw paths from the children to their pets. Point and say.
Language: cat, dog, fish, rabbit; I have a (cat).

Trace to circle the little dog's mommy. Point, ask and say.
Language: cat, dog, rabbit; mommy; Is this your mommy? Yes, it is. / No, it isn't. It's (a rabbit).

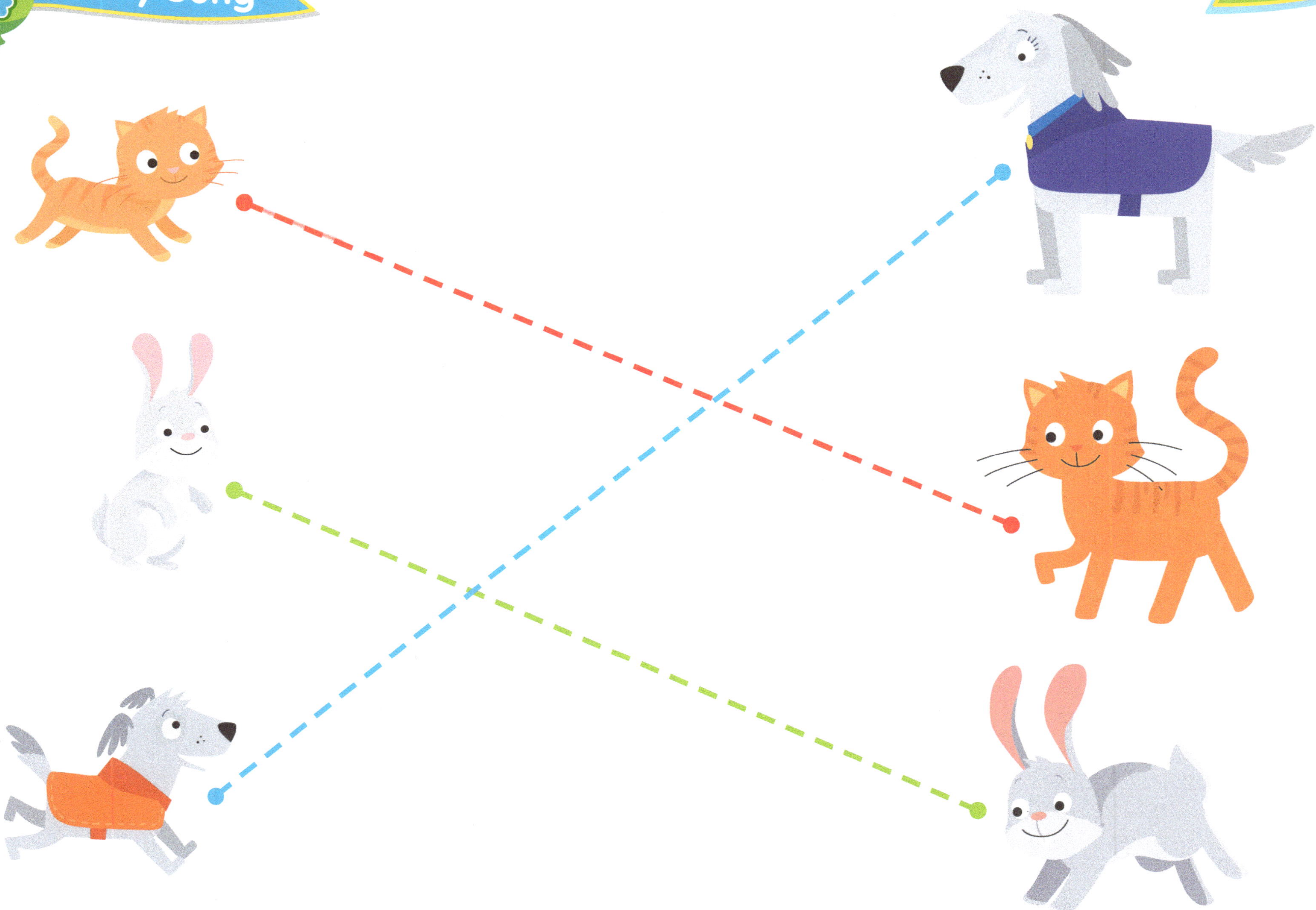

Trace to match the animals to their mommies. Point, ask and say.

Language: cat, dog, rabbit; mommy; Is this your mommy? Yes, it is. / No, it isn't. It's (a rabbit). I'm (happy).

Life skills

Trace to match the children to their pets. Color the pets. Ask and say.

Language: bird, cat, fish; blue, orange, yellow; I have a (bird). Is this your (fish)? Yes, it is. / No, it isn't. This is my (fish). My (fish) is (yellow).

Values I'm kind to you

Choose, draw and color a picture of you being kind to others. Draw your friend. Say.
Language: I'm kind to you. I help you.

SOCIAL AND EMOTIONAL LEARNING

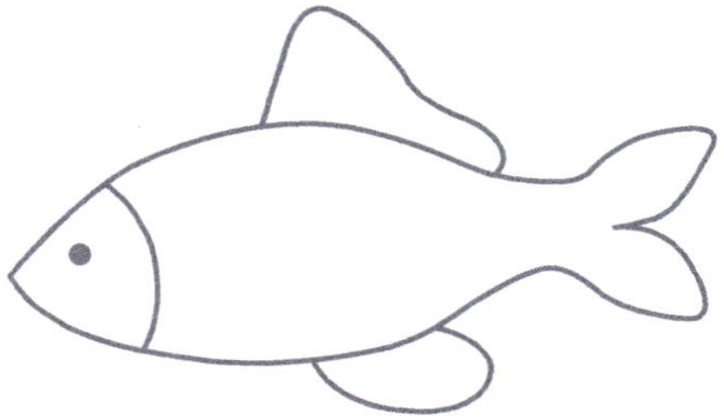

Draw the fish swimming in the water and the bird flying in the sky. Point and say.

Language: fly, swim; birds, fish; Birds fly. Fish swim.

Point and count the dots. Connect the dots in order to complete the rabbit. Color.
Language: fly, rabbit; nose; little; numbers 1–10

Color the faces to show the pets you know. Ask and say. Think and color the stars to show your progress.

Language: bird, cat, dog, fish, mouse, rabbit; I have (a mouse). Is this your (cat)? Yes, it is. / No, it isn't.

Project

Find and glue pictures of pets. Point, ask and say.

Language: bird, cat, dog, fish, mouse, rabbit; colors; Is this your (cat)? Yes, it is. / No, it isn't; I have (a mouse). What's this? It's (a bird). My (bird) is (yellow). Where's the (rabbit)? Here.

Beach

Five little crabs

Vocabulary

Lesson 1

Color the ocean blue, the sand yellow, the shell pink and the crab red. Point and say.

Language: crab, ocean, sand, shell; blue, pink, red, yellow

Find and color the bucket and the shovel. Point and say.
Language: bucket, ocean, sand, shell, shovel; I can see (a bucket). Me too.

Trace the paths to connect the story pictures in order. Color a circle to show your favorite picture in the story. Ask and say.

Language: bucket, crab, ocean, sand, shell, shovel; little; numbers 1–5; I can see (five) little crabs. Me too. How many little crabs? (Five).

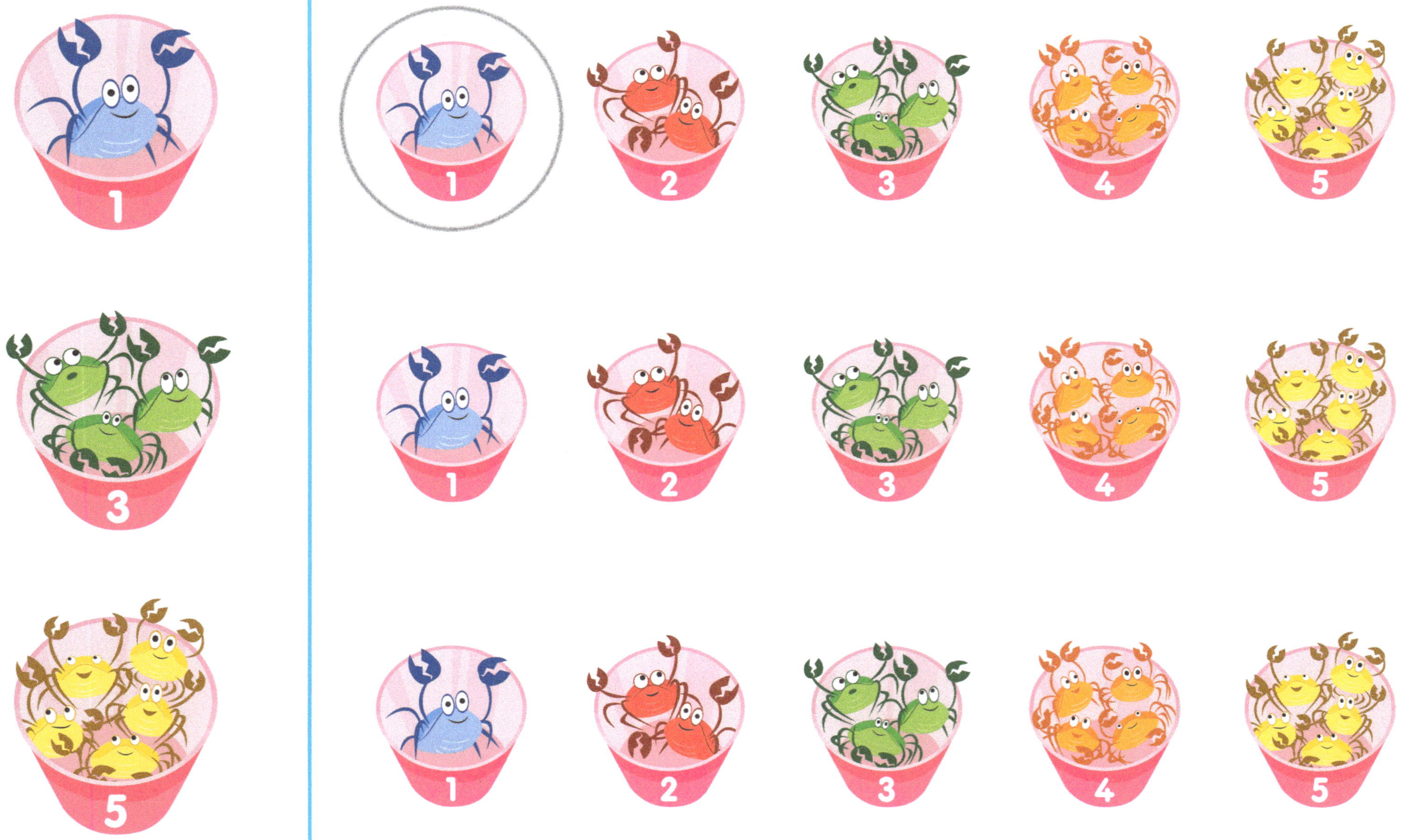

Count the crabs. Circle the picture that is the same in each row. Point, ask and say.
Language: crab; little; numbers 1–5; How many little crabs? (Five).

1 2 3 4 5 6 7 8 9 10

Color and count the shells. Circle the correct number. Ask and say.
Language: bucket, crab, ocean, sand, shell, shovel; numbers 1–10; I can see (shells). How many (shells)? (Ten). What color are the (shells)? They're (pink).

Choose, draw and color a picture of you. Say.
Language: ocean, trees; blue, green; I love the (blue) (ocean).

SOCIAL AND EMOTIONAL LEARNING

Color the animal that lives on land. Point and say.
Language: land, water; cat, fish; (Fish) live in (water). (Cats) live on (land).

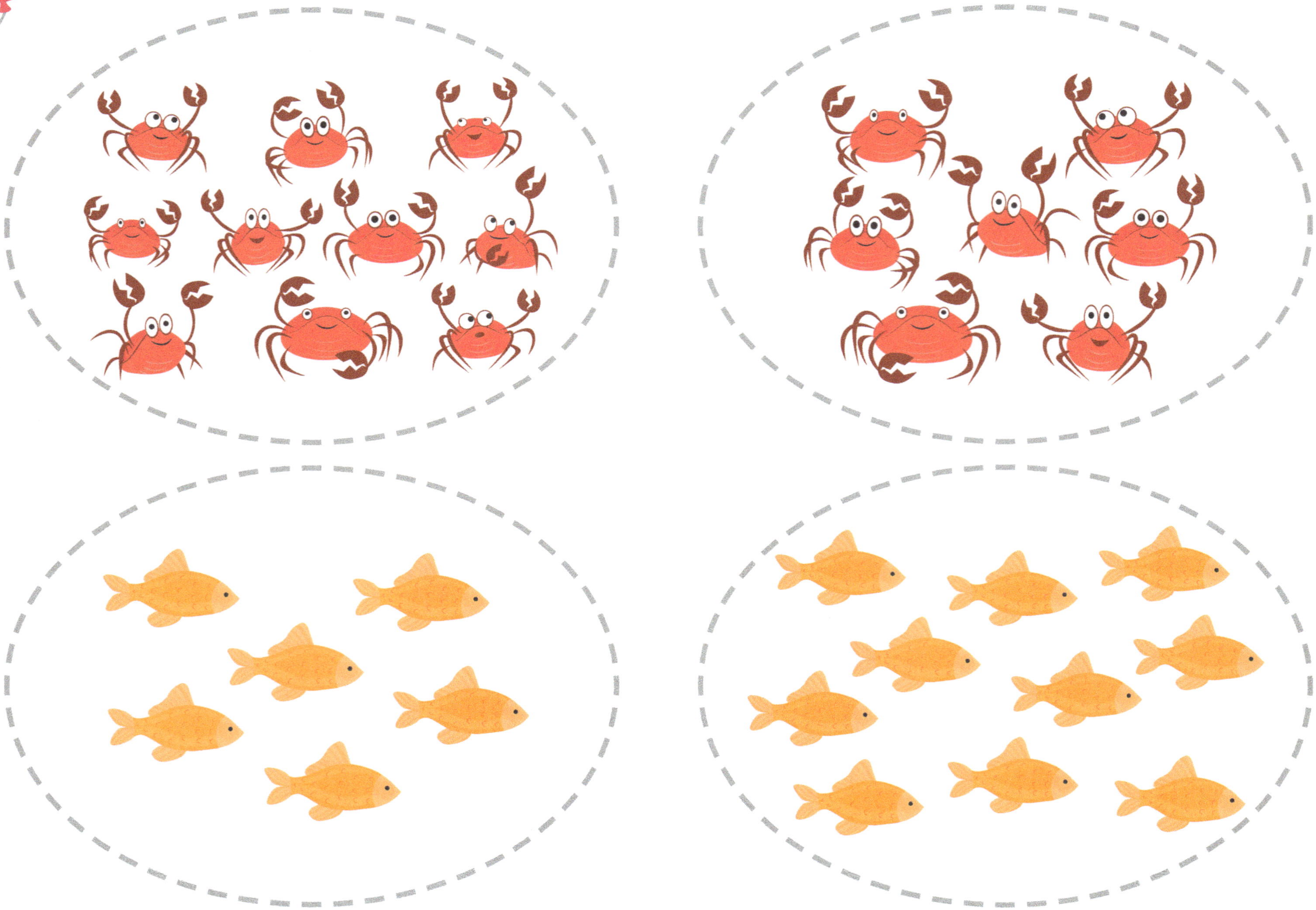

Count the crabs and the fish. Circle the pictures with ten crabs and ten fish. Point and say.
Language: crab, fish; numbers 1–10; How many (fish)? (Ten).

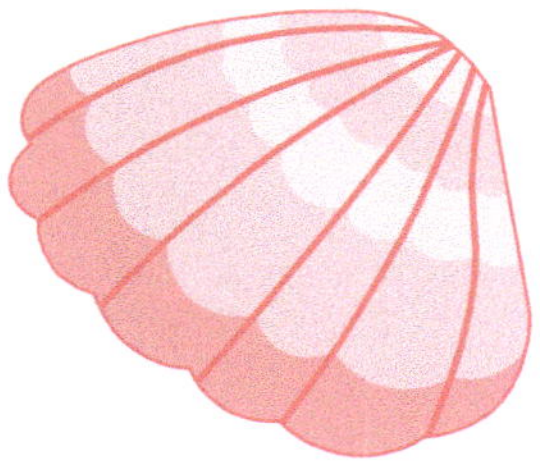
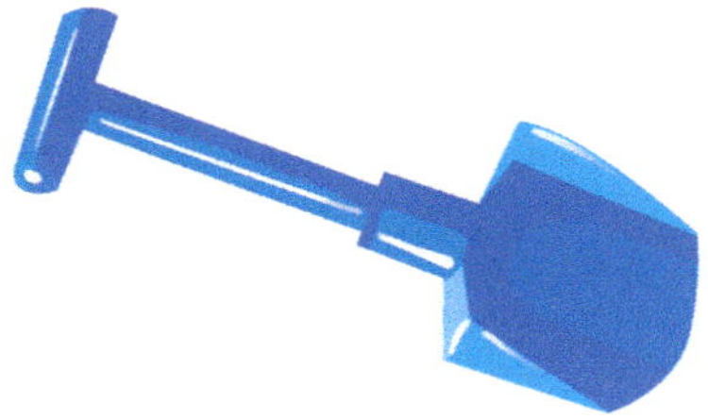

Color the faces to show the beach words you know. Ask and say. Think and color the stars to show your progress.
Language: bucket, crab, ocean, sand, shell, shovel; I can see (a bucket). Me too.

Paint a picture of the beach. Ask and say.

Language: bucket, crab, ocean, sand, shell, shovel; numbers; colors; I can see (a bucket). Me too. How many (shells)? (Three). What's this? It's (a shovel). What color are the (crabs)? They're (red).

Colors

Trace to match the children with the same color balls. Point and say.
Language: blue, green, red, yellow

Colors

Trace to circle the butterflies in the correct colors. Point and say.
Language: brown, orange, pink, purple

Numbers 1 2 3 4 5

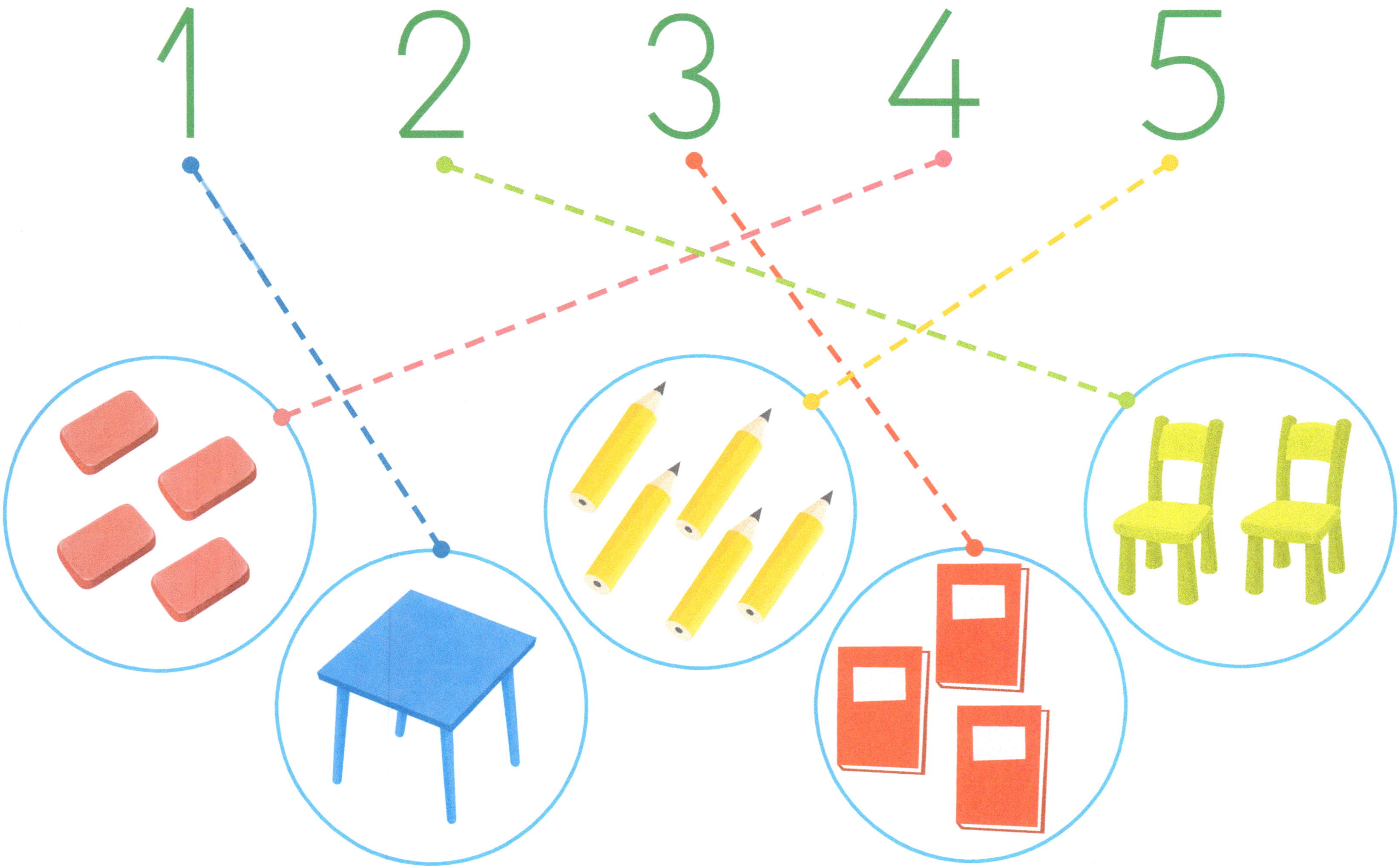

Count the objects. Trace to match the numbers to the objects. Point and say.
Language: numbers 1–5

Numbers 1 2 3 4 5 6 7 8 9 10

1
2
3
4
5

6
7
8
9
10

Trace the monster's eyes. Count the eyes and circle the correct number. Point and say.
Language: numbers 1–10

Shapes

Trace and color the next shape in each row. Point and say.
Language: circle, triangle

Shapes

Color the squares and rectangles to complete the path to the house. Point and say.
Language: rectangle, square

Concepts

Draw the mouths to show if the children are happy or sad. Point and say.
Language: happy, sad

Concepts

Color the things that are big. Circle the things that are small. Point and say.
Language: big, small

Concepts

Trace the lines to show up and down. Color the monkeys up in the trees.
Point and say. Language: up, down

Festivals

Carnival

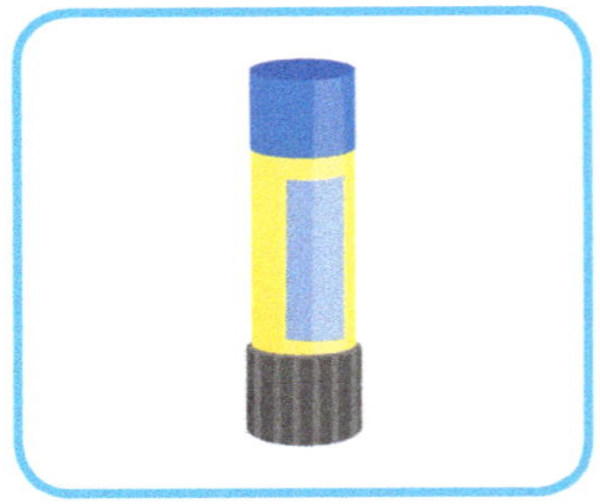

Paint and decorate your Carnival mask. Point and say.
Language: Carnival, mask; colors; Let's wear a (mask). It's (blue).

International Family Day

Find and circle five differences in the pictures. Point and say.

Language: family; mommy, daddy, grandma, grandpa, brother, sister

Festivals

Teddy Bear Day

Trace to circle the teddy bear that is the same in each row. Point and say.
Language: teddy bear; ears, eyes, feet, fur; brown